PRAYING WITH SAINT PATRICK

PRAYING WITH

SAINT
PATRICK

Prayers and Devotions Inspired by

the Irish Hero of the Faith

AARON BURNS & MATT MIKALATOS

TYNDALE
MOMENTUM®

A Tyndale nonfiction imprint

Visit Tyndale online at tyndale.com.

Visit Tyndale Momentum online at tyndalemomentum.com.

Visit the authors online at BurnsCo.us and www.mikalatos.com.

Tyndale, Tyndale's quill logo, *Tyndale Momentum*, and the Tyndale Momentum logo are registered trademarks of Tyndale House Ministries. Tyndale Momentum is a nonfiction imprint of Tyndale House Publishers, Carol Stream, Illinois.

Praying with Saint Patrick: Prayers and Devotions Inspired by the Irish Hero of the Faith

Designed by Ron C. Kaufmann

Edited by Sarah Rubio

Authors are represented by Ambassador Literary, Nashville, TN.

For information about special discounts for bulk purchases, please contact Tyndale House Publishers at csresponse@tyndale.com, or call 1-855-277-9400.

Library of Congress Cataloging-in-Publication Data

A catalog record for this book is available from the Library of Congress.

ISBN 978-1-4964-4675-6

Printed in China

30	29	28	27	26	25	24
7	6	5	4	3	2	1

To my Mom, Tracey, for instilling in me a
love for history, books, and prayer.
—Aaron

To my parents, Pete and Maggie, for their lifelong
example of praying for me and all their loved ones.
—Matt

CONTENTS

﹌❦﹌

STUDENT

SAINT

INTRODUCTION

Over a thousand years ago, a disgruntled Irish monk stole a manuscript from the shelf of a monastic library. It was eventually recovered, but when the king of Ireland heard what had happened, he was not content to let a document of such importance be left to the whim of history. So he entrusted it to the keeping of one family, christening their line MacMoyre, or "Son of the Keeper."

As the years passed, the true story contained in the document faded from memory, as hearsay, myth, and legend grew in its place. Nearly six hundred years after being entrusted with this sacred charge, the MacMoyre family fell on hard times . . . and young Florence MacMoyre pawned the manuscript for a mere £5—probably about $900 dollars today.

What, you may ask, was contained in the manuscript? The writings of Saint Patrick himself.

The Book of Armagh

When you think of Saint Patrick today, what comes to mind? A stone statue? A three-leaf clover? Perhaps green beer or green rivers? Parades with leprechauns and rainbows?

While eventually the MacMoyres' manuscript was recovered (it's called the *Book of Armagh*, and you can see it today on display in Trinity College, Dublin), the true legacy of Patrick and what God did in and through him is still lost to many of the billions who celebrate him every March 17.

Patrick lived in the transition time between the decline of the Roman Empire and the beginning of the Dark Ages. Much of this era's history has been lost forever, making what we do know about Patrick quite remarkable. The *Book of Armagh* contains copies of two letters ("Confession" and "Letter to Coroticus") that historians agree were written by Patrick himself. It also contains a prayer (called, among other titles, "Patrick's Breastplate") that is attributed to Patrick but may have been written in part by one of his later followers. In addition to these sources, we have some archaeological and corroborating historical evidence of his life and the impact of his ministry. Finally, we have many legends about this Irish hero, some that seem plausible, and others that were clearly manufactured by later churchmen or politicians seeking to build their own credibility by leaning on Patrick's legacy.

These fascinating letters and other sources reveal the outline of Patrick's story. Patrick was born not in Ireland, but in western Britain. While the exact dates and locations are unknown, a good guess is around AD 390 near modern-day Wales. We do know that his father taught him the Christian faith, which Patrick rejected. In a great raid, Irish barbarians swept down on his coastal village and carted sixteen-year-old Patrick across the Irish Sea to slavery. While tending sheep in Ireland, he turned to God, and after six years he eventually escaped back to Britain. But before long, God used a dream to call Patrick to return to the people who had enslaved him to share the love and forgiveness of Christ.

Patrick the Man

While many details of his life are missing, in Patrick's writings we meet a surprisingly relatable human, a person with struggles, disappointments, passions, and dreams—a far cry from either the stained-glass-window saint or the hard-drinking leprechaun cartoon.

Patrick was undereducated and blue collar. His writing is simple and straightforward, and he often apologizes for lacking the flowery language of his contemporaries. A rebel and a rule breaker, he was chided by his peers for paying bribes to local chieftains to protect his parishes and missionaries, declining some gifts offered to his ministry, and breaking with the Church tradition of his time by not selling priestly ordinations.

He was a man of deep desires and passions, he freely confessed that he committed major sin in his youth, and he was honest about his continuing struggles. But Patrick experienced God's forgiveness and justification, and he finished well through deep suffering, betrayal, conflict, and trials.

Patrick was illuminated with a passion for God, God's Word, and God's people. He was a man of prayer, and while his letters don't include some of the more legendary events, such as driving snakes out of Ireland, they do show God moving and working miraculously in an inspirational story of God's real power. He was steeped in Scripture—his letters overflow with scriptural references and allusions. Patrick's life was characterized by risk-taking in the service of others—particularly women, slaves, and the poor.

Patrick was one of the first cross-cultural missionaries since the apostle Paul, breaking from the prejudice of his era. Patrick's method of ministry was relational first; he adapted orthodox Christianity to Irish culture. Patrick connected the story of Christianity to the myths the Irish already believed, demonstrating the gospel's relevance to his adopted people.

Patrick's Prayers

In his "Confession," Patrick prays that his life's work would be an inspiration for future generations. This prayer was answered with a resounding *yes*, as the hundreds of churches that Patrick planted continued to expand. Historians have labeled the three centuries following Patrick "Ireland's Golden Age." The slave trade that had victimized young Patrick, as well as pagan human sacrifice, largely came to an end. Literature, art, research, and learning flourished across the island. Missionaries inspired by Patrick sailed beyond the shores of Ireland to share Christ's love with the continent of Europe, which had been devastated by barbarian raids and war.

Patrick closes the "Confession" with a prayer that anyone who hears of the amazing works that were accomplished in Ireland would not think of him but would exalt his God.

Our aim in this book is to introduce you to Patrick's writings and his story, and to inspire you to think, pray, and change the world like he did.

how to use this book

Patrick's father and grandfather were heavily involved with their church, a practice Patrick didn't think much of in his youth. But once he was enslaved in Ireland, he found himself praying all the time—praying for freedom, for a warm place to sleep, to return home, or to escape a beating. He never stopped. His life was soaked in prayer. It was something he did with great intentionality, but also in the breath between one task and the next.

In this book, we want to learn to pray with Patrick, to pray our own prayers alongside him, and to find ourselves in his story. Here are three suggestions of ways you could use this book.

1. Follow Patrick's journey day by day.

We've organized the book into four sections (Son, Slave, Student, and Saint) that follow the life of Patrick from his childhood, through his time as a slave in Ireland, then his time preparing for ministry back home in Britain, and finally his return to Ireland and long life of service as a missionary, priest, and bishop there. One option is to read this book straight through, beginning by reading Patrick's own words and then moving into the devotion and original prayer we've written inspired by his life and words.

2. Find the entry you need for today.

Patrick's life—though exceptional in many ways—was much like our lives. He had moments of anger, grief, despair, joy, and happiness. Using the entry titles in the table of contents, you can look for prayers that fit the day you are having. Need encouragement in a time of loss? Visit "A Prayer in Times of Weeping." Not sure what God is saying to you, or maybe God is saying something difficult? Read "A Prayer for When You Struggle to Accept God's Direction." Patrick had those moments, too, and we offer up our own prayers in each devotion to reflect his walk of faith.

3. Develop new prayer practices with Patrick.

There is much to be said for joining Patrick on his journey and experiencing prayer as we explore his story (like in suggestion 1). But you could also choose to read this book intentionally as a way to grow in prayer. As you read Patrick's words in each epigraph, consider ways in which Patrick's prayer life may have been different from your own. What practices did he have that you can adopt? What values did he show? What can you learn by praying the way Patrick prayed?

Our hope is that this book will draw you deeper into conversation with a God who cares deeply about you and your needs, concerns, and worries. Just as Patrick experienced God's presence in the rugged wilds of Ireland, may you experience God's presence in a powerful and vibrant way as you read this book. Blessings and peace to you.

SON

My name is Patrick. I am a sinner, a simple country person, and the least of all believers. I am looked down upon by many. My father was Calpornius. He was a deacon; his father was Potitus, a priest, who lived at Bannavem Taburniae.

PATRICK, "CONFESSION," I

A PRAYER
FOR WHEN WE DON'T HAVE
WORDS OF OUR OWN

✠

At that time, I did not know the true God.
PATRICK, "CONFESSION," I

Teach us to pray.
LUKE 11:1

Before he was a saint, Patrick was an undisciplined schoolboy. His father was a deacon in the church, and his grandfather a priest. He did not know God, did not care to know God, and the words of the priests and holy teachers—perhaps most of all those in his family—held no interest for him.

Still, his father made him sit in church and sing the songs, recite the creeds, and pray the prayers. He listened as the priests droned on in Latin. He crossed himself at the appropriate times. He stood up, sat down, bowed his knees, and filed out again to the real world, where none of these words touched him, where none of it mattered for a moment.

And though he didn't know God or believe in Christ, he was taught the ancient practices. He learned the prayer that Jesus taught his followers. He knew the pattern of the words, well worn by years of repetition, words that he did not remember learning, could not recall being taught. These words, chiseled on his heart, could not be taken away by time or hardship or slavers, a blessing that would bring him comfort in years to come.

There are times, perhaps, when we are not sure of God. We do not have the energy to cut through our own emotions to form our own thoughts, our own words to express our needs and wants to God. In those times, we can pray the words Patrick learned as a child, words that held little meaning in the moment but later became deeply important.

The followers of Jesus came to him and said, "Lord, teach us to pray." And Jesus prayed these words, the words that have been prayed by Christians in every culture and every age they have inhabited since that day:

Our Father who art in Heaven,
hallowed be Thy name.
Thy Kingdom come. Thy will be done on earth,
as it is in Heaven.
Give us this day our daily bread.
And forgive us our debts,
as we forgive our debtors.
And lead us not into temptation,
but deliver us from evil.
For Thine is the Kingdom,
and the power and the glory for ever.
Amen.[1]

A PRAYER
FOR COMPASSION
WHEN REMEMBERING OUR FAILURES

✣

I turned with all my heart to the Lord my God,
and he looked down on my lowliness and had mercy
on my youthful ignorance.
PATRICK, "CONFESSION," 2

Do not remember the rebellious sins of my youth.
Remember me in the light of your unfailing love,
for you are merciful, O LORD.
PSALM 25:7, NLT

Years later when Patrick thought back on his childhood, there were moments that made him cringe. Unkind words he had spoken that made him blush. Unwise actions that caused him to burn with shame. He, like all of us, had done things he regretted.

However, in the journey to becoming like Christ he came to realize that he must look on his youthful ignorance in the same way God did. What he had done he had done, yes, but those things were forgiven and erased, and he had been transformed. He was wiser, less impulsive, kinder, and more aware of the consequences of his own failings on himself as well as on those around him.

Still, it was hard not to look at himself with condemnation. Sins that God had forgotten Patrick remembered in vivid detail. So he was held captive not to his sin, but to the remembrance of his sin. He needed to turn his past over to God, who was more merciful than Patrick himself. On the days when his past hung heavily over him, Patrick called on God for relief.

What regrets weigh on you today? Are there words you have spoken, things you have done today or in your past for which you need forgiveness, either from yourself or others? Our merciful God offers forgiveness to all.

O Lord, you know the suffering
I have created with my own foolish behaviors.
How often I have regretted my words and my actions.
I find it hard to forgive myself,
and harder still to forget the things that I have done.
Have mercy on my ignorance.
Teach me to have compassion for myself.
I ask too, God, that you would remind me
of your unfailing love,
and teach me to love myself as you love me.

A PRAYER
OF GRATITUDE FOR OUR TEACHERS

✠

My father was Calpornius. He was a deacon;
his father was Potitus, a priest.
PATRICK, "CONFESSION," I

Remember your leaders, those who spoke to you the
word of God. Consider the outcome of their way
of life, and imitate their faith.
HEBREWS 13:7, ESV

In spite of the turbulent era he grew up in, Patrick's childhood memories were forged in a loving community. Looking back on this time, Patrick gratefully recalls his family home in the beautiful coastlands of western Britain. He was blessed with the rare gift of multiple generations—both a father and a grandfather—who loved him, mentored him, and taught him the most important things in life.

Patrick also recollects with gratitude the church community he was part of. But these gifts were not something Patrick appreciated at the time. He and his youthful friends chose to ignore their teachers: "We would not listen to our priests, who advised us about how we could be saved."[2]

But then everything changed.

As Patrick suffered as a slave, the love and truth that had been sown into his heart began to bear fruit. First it appeared in the transformation of his own life, then eventually it grew into care for others, even as he had been cared for by his community at home. Patrick carried a passion for mentoring young people throughout his life. How he would have loved an opportunity to go back and thank the people who invested in him when he was too foolish to listen.

As you reflect on your own journey, whom do you need to thank today? What names and faces come to mind of those who have poured into you? Perhaps it wasn't a parent, but a friend, colleague, pastor, or teacher. And, just as importantly, how can you find opportunities to pass along the love you have received to others?

God, thank you for filling my life
with people who truly care for me,
even when I didn't deserve it
or chose to ignore them.
Please fill me with gratitude
and empower me to find others to love
even as I have been loved.

A PRAYER
FOR TIMES OF TROUBLE

✛

At that time, I did not know the true God.
I was taken into captivity in Ireland.
PATRICK, "CONFESSION," 1

[God] decided exactly where they should live. God
did this so that people would seek him. And perhaps
they would reach out for him and find him.
ACTS 17:26-27, NIrV

Imagine the terror of being kidnapped from your homeland and packed onto a ship with hundreds of others. The cruel laughter of your captors makes their plans clear.

In the midst of that terror, Patrick didn't think of God. He didn't say, "God has this all under control." He didn't recognize his kidnapping as something from God. The fact that he did recognize it in his later life is a sign of how completely his experience changed him.

If Patrick hadn't been kidnapped, he wouldn't have learned Gaelic or met the people of Ireland. He wouldn't have done away with child sacrifice, or brought dignity to Ireland's poor, or brought new spiritual life to the island.

Patrick tells us that even when terrible things happen, God may use those things to bring good into the world, or to make us more aware of God. At the time we may not recognize God moving through the dark moments of our life. Why would we expect to? But if we adopt Patrick's hindsight about troubled times, maybe we can have our eyes opened to see God watching over us through our troubles.

God, this is a dark place. This world is full of trouble: violence and war, divorce, broken promises, loss, tears, pain, and death. There are days when I don't see you here. I have lost people I love. I have been wronged. I have been abused. I have been used. I have wondered if maybe there is no God at all. How could a God who is loving fail to step in and fix things? How could a powerful God sit on his hands?

But maybe you are doing something here. Maybe something beautiful is going to come from this all, though I admit I can't imagine how. Open my eyes to see the outline of some divine plan here. Show me that you are here with me in the dark. I want more than just comfort or hand-holding through this trouble. I need hope in the midst of this despair. I need to know that you're going to do something. I need to know that you care, and that all of this will be redeemed. Maybe in this darkness I can see your light shine brighter. Shine, Divine Presence, and show me the way to you.

slave

*After I arrived in Ireland, I tended sheep every
day, and I prayed frequently during the day.
More and more the love of God increased, and
my sense of awe before God. Faith grew, and my
spirit was moved, so that in one day I would pray
up to one hundred times, and at night perhaps
the same. I even remained in the woods and on
the mountain, and I would rise to pray before
dawn in snow and ice and rain. I never felt the
worse for it, and I never felt lazy—as I realise
now, the spirit was burning in me at that time.*

PATRICK, "CONFESSION," 16

A PRAYER
FOR WHEN WE FEEL HELPLESS

It was among foreigners that it was seen
how little I was.
PATRICK, "CONFESSION," I

I am utterly helpless.
JOB 6:13, NLT

There was nothing to be done, no way for Patrick to save himself. Home was gone, lost in the waves behind them. He had been packed into the boat with the others, and he couldn't escape. He was beaten, kicked, pushed into the mud. His clothes were taken from him. The slavers spoke to him in rough Latin, then in Gaelic, and soon he found himself living in a makeshift hut, cold, miserable, hungry, and naked. He couldn't understand anyone, let alone communicate.

All his life he had been the deacon's son. He had scarcely been cold in his life, had never been truly hungry. Now he lived in cowering fear. There was a time when he had been full of pride, despite his inability to love himself. Now, in the mud and cold, all of the fine things he thought about himself had proven themselves false. He was not strong enough to break free. Not smart enough to find a way home. Not brave enough to stand up to his new master.

We have all found ourselves in a place where we do not have the resources to solve our problems. There are things we cannot fix. Injustices that defeat us no matter how passionately we oppose them. In those times we come to realize how small we are, how helpless. Like Patrick, we recognize that we need something more than ourselves—someone greater to reach into our lives and pull us to freedom. We may be small, but God cares even for the smallest creatures of the earth. He keeps an eye on the sparrows—and you are worth more than many sparrows.

God, I am utterly helpless. I am small. All my strength, my intelligence, my money, my relationships can't get me out of this mess. I am suffering. Do you see me here? Do you hear my words? If you do, God, I know you are not helpless. You are not small. Please, hear my prayer. Show me a sign today that you see me here in my weakness. Let me know that you are listening when I cry out to you.

A PRAYER
FOR AN INCREASE IN OUR LOVE FOR GOD

✠

After I arrived in Ireland, I tended sheep every day,
and I prayed frequently during the day. More and
more the love of God increased, and my sense
of awe before God.
PATRICK, "CONFESSION," 16

There is no fear in love. But perfect love drives out
fear, because fear has to do with punishment.
I JOHN 4:18

atrick's new master, Milchu, carried him off to tend sheep in the rugged forests of western Ireland, far from home and hope. Patrick could have cursed God, but instead he took all that had happened as evidence God was trying to get his attention. God was calling Patrick, asking him to follow.

Morning and night, Patrick walked among the sheep, guiding them, guarding them, leading them. Throughout the day, Patrick prayed. Every day that passed he prayed more, and his love for God increased. Which caused him to pray more. Which deepened his love.

He prayed on the mountain and in the deep woods. He woke early, before the sheep, and he prayed.

In his youth, Patrick had ignored God, ignored the priests, ignored the Scriptures, and ignored his parents—but now he worked to remember the smallest scraps of Scripture, the half-remembered melody of a hymn, the last few phrases of a liturgy.

He clung to these things like the words of a distant beloved. He began to see that God was not distant. God was there, in the sunlight and rain and snow. Behind and above, around and below. The sheep, the trees, the grass, all were reminders of God. So it was that there in Ireland—a slave in a land with no church, no Bible, no priest—Patrick found himself falling in love at last with God. So what could he do other than pray?

God is more powerful and loving than we can imagine. As our relationship with God grows through honest conversation, we too can experience peace and security, even in uncertain and difficult times.

Teach me to love you, Lord. So often I think of prayer as an obligation, or something I turn to in moments of fear or need. I want it to be something more. I want it to be the deep communication of my soul to you. Teach me to be eager to pray. Change my heart so I desire more prayer in my life. Connect me to you, fill me up with your presence. And lead me in the everlasting way. Remind me today to pray in the moments in between, and open my eyes to see you in the everyday.

a prayer
for our daily needs

✠

I was . . . brought low by hunger
and nakedness daily.
PATRICK, "CONFESSION," 27

Do not worry about your life, what you will eat or
drink; or about your body, what you will wear.
Is not life more than food, and the body
more than clothes?
MATTHEW 6:25

"**F**eed my sheep."

That was Patrick's job. Take care of the lambs. But who took care of him? No one. The barest crust of bread. A hovel to sleep in. The sheep to keep him warm. And he was still cold, yes. Cold rain in the fall and spring, and snow often enough in the winter, and he without shoes and too often without clothing.

In those days, Patrick took to praying. As he moved the sheep along so they could find food, he found himself caring for them despite it all. Not for his master, no, but for the sheep. And if he cared this little bit for the sheep—he, Patrick, who had never once cared for anyone but himself—then surely God, the God of his father and grandfather, might care for Patrick?

He remembered his father telling him once not to worry about tomorrow, that today had enough worries. Those were the words of Jesus, his father had told him. So Patrick set himself to pray, to care for his sheep, to listen for the voice of God. He couldn't bring himself bread. He couldn't make himself clothes. But he could—at least he was learning how to—rely on God to bring him those things.

Like Patrick, we may not be able to feed ourselves. We may not know where the next paycheck is coming from. We may not be able to replace worn-out clothes or repair the car if it breaks. But Patrick came to understand that whether we are rich or poor, whether there is plenty or just enough, it is God who provides.

*Lord God, I don't want to spend my life worrying.
Life is more than the food we eat and the clothes
we wear, and you know we need these things.
Help me to trust in you. And please, God, give us
today our daily bread. Not too much, so we forget
our need of you. Not too little, so that I steal and
disgrace your name. But please, God, please, give
me enough for today.*

A PRAYER
FOR GROWTH THROUGH THE HARD TIMES

✠

*I remained on in Ireland, and that not of my own
choosing, until I almost perished. However, it was
very good for me, since God straightened me out,
and he prepared me for what I would be today.*
PATRICK, "CONFESSION," 28

*Suffering produces endurance, and endurance
produces character, and character produces hope.*
ROMANS 5:3-4, ESV

s the weeks stretched into months, young Patrick's
last hopes faded. No rescue was coming from
home. No Irishman would listen to his pleas for
justice. Miles from the coast, with no understanding of the
local language or customs, escape was impossible.

But somehow, in all of this, God was still at work.

Separated from everything he was used to depending on,
a broken and humbled Patrick began an otherwise impossible spiritual journey. God used the very circumstances that

crushed Patrick to transform him into a man who would eventually transform his world.

As we look at Scripture, this is a pattern that we see repeatedly. Think of Moses in the book of Exodus, and King David in the book of 1 Samuel. God used the trial of herding sheep in the desert while running from their enemies to mold and shape both of them into heroes of faith—and he did something similar for Patrick.

In the midst of trials, we often find it impossible to see beyond the moment. It is hard to imagine that any good could come out of unimaginably bad circumstances. Miscarriage. Bankruptcy. Cancer. Betrayal. Addiction. Some trials are of our own making, some from the cursed world we live in, and some from people who intentionally sin against us. Each of these is a tragedy. But do we believe that our God is able to take something that is truly bad and use it to shape us for his purposes?

Lord, I am going through a lot right now. This circumstance is painful in every way imaginable. It's not what I asked for and not what I had planned. In the midst of this suffering, would you grow in me an enduring dependence on you? Would you mold me into someone who can be used by you? Would you fill me with hope? And in the years to come, would you allow me to see how your loving hand was guiding me through it all?

A PRAYER
FOR HOPE

It was there one night in my sleep that I heard a voice saying to me: "You have fasted well. Very soon you will return to your native country." Again after a short while, I heard someone saying to me: "Look—your ship is ready."

PATRICK, "CONFESSION," 17

We look forward with hope to that wonderful day.

TITUS 2:13, NLT

The young shepherd woke, but he remembered the voice clearly. "You have fasted well. Very soon you will return to your native country." No instructions, no details, just "soon you will return." *Soon you will return!*

This changed everything. His freezing, ramshackle hut to keep off the rain, the filthy rags he wore, the endless call of hungry sheep in the morning: none of it mattered. It was time to walk through the fields and woods, time to climb the mountain with his flock. But Patrick couldn't help but notice the glimmer of sun piercing the dark clouds. Laughter bubbled up from his chest and out of his mouth.

In some sense, nothing had changed. He had no idea how he would be returning home. "Soon" might be a month or . . . a hundred months. Didn't Scripture say that a day is like a thousand years and a thousand years a day to the Lord?[3] His return could be years away.

Still, Patrick set about his day's work with an unshakable feeling of joy. The sun was there, behind those clouds. The presence of the clouds did not change that. And his captivity meant little in the face of God's words to him: *Soon you will be free!*

Hope does not change our circumstances, but it gives us power over them. Our current troubles will not last forever! Hope gives me strength to work toward something better, and perseverance to handle the worst things, knowing that in time this, too, shall pass.

God, thank you for speaking to me—through the world around me, through my friends, through your words in Scripture, and yes, in prayer. Your every word is a promise. I know that when you say you will free me from captivity, or that you will bring me home, or that good things are coming, I don't need to waste time wondering if that's true. It is true! If I could see what was coming, how would that be hope? If I knew how you would do it, that wouldn't be hope either. But now I feel the unmistakable certainty that you are doing something wonderful. Thank you for telling me ahead of time, so I could look forward to it! Thank you for giving me this ray of sunlight on this dark and stormy day.

A PRAYER
FOR FREEDOM

✛

It was not nearby, but a good two hundred miles
away. I had never been to the place, nor did I know
anyone there. So I ran away then, and left the man
with whom I had been for six years.
PATRICK, "CONFESSION," 17

Those who hope in the LORD
will renew their strength.
They will soar on wings like eagles;
they will run and not grow weary,
they will walk and not be faint.
ISAIAH 40:31

W hen the instructions came from God, Patrick
might have expected something simpler.
Maybe his parents walking up the sheep path,
a squad of Roman soldiers behind them. A boat left untied
nearby. His master writing him a certificate of freedom.

Instead, when the word of the Lord came, it was through

a vision of a place two hundred miles away, a place Patrick didn't know. He would have to go on foot. He walked miles each day with the sheep, so the thought of the distance didn't bother him much—it was the amount of time it would take. Weeks alone on the road, without friends, maybe without food, and possibly with the man who owned him chasing him along the way.

But Patrick had learned not to doubt God. If God said Patrick was going home and if the place he had seen in his dream was the place to do it, then he had no questions. He picked up his walking staff and started walking. He passed his flock, his little hovel, and the house where the man who had been his master for the last six years lived. He kept walking onward, without looking back.

Where are you feeling trapped in life? Is God showing you a way out, even if it is far off? The Scriptures say it is for freedom that we have been set free![4] It's time to walk away from your captivity and embrace the path homeward.

Redemption! God, I have been bought once before by another master, and these long years I've been serving, unable to escape. But now you have shown me another way out. Give me strength for this journey. Give me energy for the walk. Give me courage for the escape, and most of all, God, please redeem me from this captivity I've been trapped in. Show me the way to freedom. Give me perseverance to follow the path you set out, no matter how many miles it is, and no matter how long it takes.

A PRAYER
FOR PROTECTION

✦

It was in the strength of God that I went—God
who turned the direction of my life to good; I feared
nothing while I was on the journey to that ship.
PATRICK, "CONFESSION," 17

Many are saying of me,
"God will not deliver him."
But you, LORD, are a shield around me,
my glory, the One who lifts my head high.
PSALM 3:2-3

No doubt there was hardship, hunger, blisters, pain, and thirst along the path. The one thing Patrick did not experience, he tells us, was fear. He didn't fear wild beasts or human beings, he didn't fear hunger or the elements, he didn't fear that he had misheard the words of God.

He knew that "perfect love casts out fear,"[5] and these last six years he had grown in his understanding of what God's love was. So he continued the journey, one foot in front of the other. He slept when a safe or dry or warm place provided itself. He accepted what kindness he could from those along the way who took pity on him.

It was the sort of trek he would not have imagined six years ago, before he knew himself. Back then he had been weak in spirit and body, and now both had grown, had strengthened. In his own strength he would have been defeated. He would have been terrified. But despite it all, being kidnapped from his home had turned his life toward good. So what did he have to fear? This path of obeying the voice of God had brought him only good things.

When God calls us to difficult or even impossible things, it's our track record with him that makes us believe that it could be possible. When he calls us to hard things in our present, we remind ourselves of his faithfulness in the past.

Lord God, anyone with a shred of sense would look at this road and say it was impossible. "That can't be God saying that to you. Where will you sleep? The road is far, and you have no friends along the way. Are you sure it was God speaking?" But I'm sure it was you, and you've promised good things if I follow. So protect me as I walk this path you've shown me. Remind me of your goodness, and remind me of your track record: you've never let me down once. Keep me safe and keep me from fear. And help me to see you along the road.

a prayer
of thanks for answered prayer

✣

*When I heard that, I left them and went back
to the hut where I had lodgings. I began to pray
while I was going; and before I even finished the
prayer, I heard one of them shout aloud at me:
"Come quickly—those men are calling you!"*
PATRICK, "CONFESSION," 18

*I will give you thanks, for you answered me;
you have become my salvation.*
PSALM 118:21

hen Patrick arrived at the port, the captain of
the ship said there was no way Patrick could
come with them. But Patrick didn't give up.
He went to pray, and just like that, it was done. Before he
had even finished his prayer—not that he was given to short
prayers—one of the sailors was shouting for him: "Come
quickly, the captain has changed his mind. We will trust you.
We will take you home."

What joy filled Patrick's heart! He was reminded of the old proverb that said the heart of the king is like a watercourse in the Lord's hand, and that God directs that water wherever he pleases.[6] The authority of a sea captain means little before the authority of the God who made the sea.

So Patrick ran for the ship and climbed aboard, and soon there was the sound of sailors shouting to one another, ropes being tossed on deck, and the gentle motion of the ship as it pushed away from shore. For the first time in six years, Patrick's feet no longer stood on the soil of Ireland. He was free.

Let us, like Patrick, turn our memories for a few moments to the times that God has answered our prayers.

O Lord, you've answered my prayers! Prayers that I would be released from captivity. Prayers that I would no longer be a slave. Prayers that I would be returned home, that I would be safe on my journey, that I would have food and shelter and protection and favor. Now, here, on this day, at last so many of those prayers are all answered in this one moment, and I am filled with joy. Thank you! Thank you that you always hear me, and that you always know my needs! Thank you for releasing me from this part of my life and into another! All praise to you, all thanks to you, and may your name be blessed.

A PRAYER
FOR THE HOPE OF CHRIST
TO COME TO OTHERS

✣

*They were pagans, and I hoped they might come
to faith in Jesus Christ. This is how I got to go
with them, and we set sail right away.*
PATRICK, "CONFESSION," 18

*The Spirit of the Sovereign LORD is on me,
because the LORD has anointed me
to proclaim good news to the poor.*
ISAIAH 61:1

I n his deep thankfulness, it was only natural that
Patrick's first thought would be to share the good
news of his God with those who had been instru-
mental in his escape. So he told them his whole story: How
he had been kidnapped from his home. How he had been a
slave in Ireland, a shepherd.

He told them how they had been an answer to his prayers.
Patrick had prayed, and God had sent them to the exact

place, at exactly the right time, to be his vehicle of salvation. He told them how God had told him where and when to meet them weeks ago, that God had been moving them to that port at the same time he was moving Patrick.

He told them that they, too, could know this wonderful God—Jesus Christ—who brought good news to the poor and freedom for captives, who could command the waves as well as the hearts of captains and sailors. Nothing could stop him from telling them his story, such was the joy that overflowed from his heart.

Who has God brought into your life? Someone who doesn't know God? And what about your story would be good news about Jesus to them? Let's pray that God would give us boldness and honesty as we tell the true story of the amazing things God has done for us.

O Lord, I can't keep my mouth shut. The people around me don't always want to hear it, but I can't stop talking about you and the wonderful things you've done. It's such good news! So wonderful how you care for us, how you intervene in our lives to bring good things! How could I keep silent, then? How unloving would I have to be to keep this secret from the people around me? Help me to be bold, as I should, and honest, as you desire, as I tell people the good news about the Word of Life.

a homecoming
prayer

✛

*I was again with my parents in Britain. They
welcomed me as a son, and they pleaded with
me that, after all the many tribulations I had
undergone, I should never leave them again.*
PATRICK, "CONFESSION," 23

*Lord, through all the generations
you have been our home!*
PSALM 90:1, NLT

hen, after all Patrick had been through, to find
himself home.

Patrick's heart stretched tight with emotions
as he walked through the village, seeing things that were the
same, noticing things that were different—burned homes
and buildings that had never been rebuilt, scars on people
who had none before the raid. Tears stung his eyes as he
noticed the spire of his grandfather's church rising above the

houses, as he saw the cross over all, as it should be. Years ago he had felt anger, obligation, and frustration when he came close to that building, and now he felt only overwhelming thankfulness.

He'd never written a letter home—how could he? He'd sent no message other than his prayers. They didn't know he was coming, they hadn't prepared a room for him, there was no homecoming dinner boiling in the pot when he came to the door. He knocked, which he had never done before, but this was no longer his house.

Then the door opened and his mother stood before him and there were only screams of joy, tears, hugs, someone from the house running to fetch his father, and then more hugs, kisses, holy embraces, his parents hovering near him as if he would disappear, sitting near him, his mother pausing to touch his shoulder as she bustled around the kitchen preparing a meal.

He was home. The warm fire, the comfortable chair, a bowl of fresh stew in his hands, an old blanket over his shoulders, his parents sitting close as he told them the story, as he shared his life with them late into the night.

He had nearly forgotten what a home was these last six years. He could not imagine ever leaving home again.

How far are you from home today? If close to home, then join Patrick in a prayer of thanks! If far from home, pray that you'll find your home in God.

There are times when my only home has been with you, God. And times when I find home among friends or family on this earth. Either way, what can I say? I can only thank you so many times. Nevertheless, I am thankful. You have given me freedom and food and a roof over my head. You have broken my chains. I have, at last, run out of words. I can only say what I have said so many times already: thank you, thank you, thank you!

STUDENT

*A few years later I was again with my
parents in Britain. They welcomed me as a
son, and they pleaded with me that, after
all the many tribulations I had undergone,
I should never leave them again.*
PATRICK, "CONFESSION," 23

*I am not telling lies: from the time in my youth
that I came to know him, the love and reverence
for God grew in me, and so far, with the
Lord's help, I have kept faith.*
PATRICK, "CONFESSION," 44

A PRAYER
FOR KNOWLEDGE AND LOVE OF GOD

✠

Where did such a great and life-giving gift come
from then, to know and love God, even at the
cost of leaving homeland and parents?
PATRICK, "CONFESSION," 36

Taste and see that the LORD is good;
blessed is the one who takes refuge in him.
PSALM 34:8

In pagan slavery Patrick had grown in his love for God without a church, without Scripture, and without instruction. He had the memory of what he'd been taught in his youth. He had snatches of half-remembered hymns and sermons. He had the glow of the moon at night, the sound of the wind through the patched roof of his hut, the bleating of the lambs, and come morning the warm light glinting on the emerald grass. He read about God in the book of nature, and the more he knew God, the more he loved God.

Now Patrick was home again, and what luxury! His father, his mother, and his grandfather were all followers of Christ with decades of knowledge. A treasure trove of books in his native tongue were all within reach. There were daily services in the church, confession and Communion available to all, and more priests and deacons within an hour's walk than in the whole of Ireland.

Patrick felt a hunger, a yearning to know God. And what better place than here?

Our relationship with God is like any other. We can be acquaintances, or friends, or closer than family. Much of it depends on how much time we spend together, on how hard we work to get to know God (who already knows us better than we know ourselves!). And like any friendship, there's nothing wrong with saying, "I want to know you better!"

O God, teach me about you! On you, on your law I meditate day and night. When I lie down, it's you I think about. When I get up in the morning, I thank you for the new day and eagerly anticipate knowing you better. The more I know you, the more I love you. The more I love you, the more I want to know you. Thank you for this place, where there are so many tools to get to know you better. Not just nature but also books and music and church services and people who have known you longer than I have been alive. Show me how to know you more! Teach me how to love you more deeply!

A PRAYER
FOR WHEN YOU DON'T FIT IN

✛

Who was it who called one as foolish as I am
from the middle of those who are seen to be
wise and experienced in law and powerful
in speech and in everything?
PATRICK, "CONFESSION," 13

God makes a home for the lonely.
PSALM 68:6, NASB

Old friends were married now, their children trailing them around the village. Relationships had shifted, new jokes had been told, new friendships cemented, and there was only so much reminiscing about old times anyone could do.

Patrick quickly decided to enter the Church and study to be a minister, but if he expected to immediately be at home there, he was disappointed. His Latin was that of a child—one who had not paid particularly close attention in school. He struggled to keep up with his peers, who had been studying while he herded sheep.

And of course, none of them woke screaming in the night, drenched in sweat, terrified that they were on that boat again, or that they would wake in a slave's hovel across the sea. While his classmates complained about school assignments and other responsibilities, Patrick knew this life of candlelit study and church chores was one of luxury.

Patrick was alone in a way that tasted bittersweet compared to his loneliness on the hills of Ireland. He was alone among friends, among his classmates, even in his family. It was a loneliness that came because of who he was—a loneliness that he didn't expect would ever leave him.

Maybe you, too, sometimes feel like the person who is furthest behind in class. Or perhaps you feel lonely even among friends, and you don't know why. There may have been times you felt trapped or abandoned. You may have experienced loss that others—who have not yet felt that sting—cannot understand.

All around me there are people living a different sort of life. They are happy while I stare at a wall, caught up in my own memories, my own worries. They are laughing when, at times, I struggle to smile. Sometimes when they complain about small things, I find myself filled with thankfulness for how small these problems are compared to those in my past. God, remind me that you're with me. Remind me that I may be by myself but I'm never alone. And, if it pleases you, maybe you could use the unique path my life has taken to help me bring your message to those who do not know you.

A PRAYER
TO BE OF HELP

✠

*I saw, in a vision in the night, a man . . . coming
as it were from Ireland with so many letters they
could not be counted. He gave me one of these, and
I read the beginning of the letter, the voice of the
Irish people. . . . They called out as it were with one
voice: "We beg you, holy boy, to come and walk again
among us." This touched my heart deeply, and I
could not read any further; I woke up then.*
PATRICK, "CONFESSION," 23

*During the night Paul had a vision of a man of
Macedonia standing and begging him, "Come over to
Macedonia and help us." After Paul had seen the vision,
we got ready at once to leave for Macedonia, concluding
that God had called us to preach the gospel to them.*
ACTS 16:9-10

The vision came when Patrick was sleeping in his childhood home, in his childhood bed. A man bearing an endless supply of letters. Thousands of letters, each one speaking with the voice of the Irish, sharing one request: begging Patrick to return, to come and bring the bright words of the holy God back to them. Patrick began to read, but he couldn't get through even a single letter. He was too deeply moved by the chorus of voices.

He awoke to a wave of emotion, drowning him in his bed. The first thing he felt was not joy or regret at the thought of leaving home or fear of returning to Ireland. It was a deep compassion for these poor souls calling out to him through this dream, these enslaved, hungry and thirsty masses who did not know Christ.

But Patrick did know Christ.

And he knew those people of Ireland too. He had walked among them.

He did not feel uncertainty about what was being asked of him.

Like Patrick, God may bring to mind a person or people who do not know Jesus. It may be someone from your past or someone from your present. What if they, like the people of Ireland, are asking for you to come and show them what is true?

O Lord, what can I say? I have seen a great need in the world around me. My heart aches for these people. I only have five words to pray today, my Lord: "Here am I. send me!"

A PRAYER
FOR WHEN YOU STRUGGLE TO ACCEPT
GOD'S DIRECTION

✠

I was not quick to accept what he showed me,
and so the Spirit prompted me.
PATRICK, "CONFESSION," 46

Not my will, but yours be done.
LUKE 22:42

It was not only returning to Ireland. The thought of that could make him nauseous. But maybe worse was the thought of leaving his family. He had new dreams, too, of serving God here in his own homeland. Though it was clear that God had spoken to him, God had not spoken to Patrick's friends. God had not spoken to Patrick's superiors in the Church. God had not spoken to Patrick's parents.

So it was easy, sometimes, to pretend that God had not

spoken. Yes, there had been a vision and the voices of the Irish asking him to come back, calling to him from across the sea. But the passing days could make them seem distant and quiet.

Then he would be studying the Scriptures by the light of a candle, or scrubbing out a pot after the communal meal, or watching over the monastery's sheep, and the still small voice of the Spirit would prompt him. Poke him. Remind him.

He knew what God had showed him, and it didn't matter that his superiors had not seen it. He knew what God was asking from him, and it didn't matter that God hadn't told his parents the same thing. He knew what God wanted, but he wasn't sure that he, Patrick, wanted the same thing.

There is a time for wise counsel, and Patrick knew that well. There is a time to listen to one's elders and one's superiors, and Patrick did that. In time they would come to see what he already knew: God had set out a path for him. Sometimes this is true for us, too, and the question that remains is simple: Will we follow?

Dearest Jesus, I know what you are asking from me, but I find myself daydreaming about another path. I am struggling to accept what you have shown me. There is a sacrifice to follow where you are leading. I want another path than the one you are directing me down. I am not quick to accept what you are saying, so please, Spirit, prompt me. Remind me. Show me again what you are asking. And give me the strength to say, "Not my will, but yours be done."

A PRAYER
TO SEE OTHERS THE WAY GOD SEES THEM

✠

It is right that we should fish well and diligently,
as the Lord directs and teaches.
PATRICK, "CONFESSION," 40

I will say to those who were not My people,
"You are My people!"
HOSEA 2:23, NASB

Ireland was full of slavers. Not just slavers, but cruel masters, people who had given Patrick no shelter, no affection, no care. In addition, the Irish often killed their children, sacrificing them to vindictive gods in the hopes that next season there would be more favorable weather and better crops, a banner year.

Back home now, Patrick studied the ancient words of God in cheery candlelight or in the sunshine of his parents' atrium. He was well fed, well rested, fully clothed, and even warm in winter by the crackling fire. It was easy to see his time in Ireland as a nightmare, a distant and dark dream that had passed and should be set aside.

And yet the words of Scripture kept reminding him of God's heart for those who were lost. Jesus said, "Go and teach all nations."[7] *All nations, but surely not the slavers of Ireland.* "Go into all the world." *But not Ireland, Lord, surely not there.* "Announce the gospel to every creature."[8] Why did these words pierce Patrick's heart? "In the place where it was said, 'You are not my people,' there they will be called children of the living God."[9]

They are not my people, Patrick said to himself. And the Word of God echoed back, "They will be called children of the living God." Patrick couldn't avoid the tragic thought that both Ireland's slavers and its slaves, both parents and poor sacrificed babies— they were all children. Children who had no idea a divine Father wanted to take them into his loving arms.

We have all been wounded by other human beings—some of us in truly horrific ways, as bad as (or even worse) than what Patrick experienced. Could God help us to see them as he sees them? To pray even for those people?

O God, help me. There are many evil people in the world, many I want to see as villains. Help me to see them as something more. To know their evil actions are harming them as well as the people around them. Give me compassion for these poor storm-tossed children of yours. Bring to mind those I hate, and remind me that all people of flesh and blood are loved by you. And give me strength to be the one to tell them that there is a better way.

A PRAYER
FOR SEASONS OF WAITING

It is there that I await his promise.
PATRICK, "CONFESSION," 39

I wait for the LORD, my soul waits,
and in his word I hope;
my soul waits for the Lord
more than watchmen for the morning.
PSALM 130:5-6, ESV

rom our vantage point, Patrick appears to be a man of action. A hero who boldly accomplished great missions for his King. But in reality, Patrick spent the first half of his life . . . waiting.

As a youth, he yearned to be old enough to rid himself of his father's rules. As a slave, he waited six years to find freedom. Now safely home, in a twist of irony, Patrick longed for the opportunity to return to Ireland. God had called him to go, but the months slipped into years, with no support for his mission materializing.

When we are in the midst of a hard trial, we endure, we press on with hope of resolution. When we are faced with a challenging task, we summon our courage and conquer. But when we are called simply to wait, how can we keep our faith alive? Waiting and the uncertainty it brings can be the cruelest crucible of suffering. Yes, we are aware that God's timing is not our timing, but it's incredibly painful.

As Patrick waited in faith, he continued to pray toward the future, without neglecting to faithfully minister in the present. And he was careful to watch for the hand of the Lord shaping both his circumstances and his own character.

What are you praying for today? A relationship, a job, a home, an opportunity? Relief from a trial? Healing, physical or spiritual, for yourself or a loved one? Cling to the truth that your heavenly Father has good plans for you, and prepare to be amazed at his grace when the timing is right.

O God, give me patience! I'm struggling to be content where I am instead of where I will someday be. I know there are ways I need to grow, things that must be done in preparation. Help me to focus on the present and trust you. From my point of view it seems best if we do this new thing starting tomorrow, but I know that you are far wiser than me. You know all things. Give me patience to enjoy watching your plan unfold.

SAINT

I saw, in a vision in the night, a man whose name was Victoricus coming as it were from Ireland with so many letters they could not be counted. He gave me one of these, and I read the beginning of the letter, the voice of the Irish people. While I was reading out the beginning of the letter, I thought I heard at that moment the voice of those who were beside the wood of Voclut, near the western sea. They called out as it were with one voice: "We beg you, holy boy, to come and walk again among us." This touched my heart deeply, and I could not read any further; I woke up then. Thanks be to God, after many years the Lord granted them what they were calling for.

PATRICK, "CONFESSION," 23

A PRAYER
IN THE MIDST OF MORTAL DANGER

✠

*Every day there is the chance that I will be killed, or
surrounded, or be taken into slavery, or some other
such happening. But I fear none of these things,
because of the promises of heaven.*
PATRICK, "CONFESSION," 55

*Even though I walk through the valley
of the shadow of death,
I will fear no evil,
for you are with me.*
PSALM 23:4, ESV

s soon as his feet touched the Irish beach, his
old life came flooding back. He had been freed
from slavery once, but there was no guarantee
Patrick would remain free. His priestly garments would not
discourage an Irish slave master in need of more product.
Patrick, his companions, and whatever Irish converts the
Lord blessed them with—all would be in danger of being

enslaved, robbed, or even murdered. God had called him here. But it was not safe. God didn't promise health or wealth or even food, shelter, warmth, and companionship.

But fear had fallen away. He found that his heart no longer pounded against his chest, his hands did not sweat or tremble, his voice didn't quaver anymore when one of the Irish—whether king or brigand—threatened him.

What had changed?

Only that Patrick saw now that in heaven there would be no hunger, no cold winter nights, no tears, no shame. There was no cause to fear in any of those things.

On those rare days when he felt fear creeping in again, he prayed that God would remove all those thoughts of pain and suffering and replace them with the knowledge that God was here beside him. He asked that his love for the Irish people would banish his fear.

So much of our fear is rooted in fear of death. Chemotherapy or viruses, venomous spiders or snakes, thieves or dark alleys, or a hundred thousand other things. We can be freed from those fears. We can know that God is beside us. We can ask God to show us, to remind us.

Lord and Master, God of all, remind me you are near. I'm in danger, and I'm afraid. The poet sang of the "valley of the shadow of death," and that shadow has fallen on me today. I don't ask for courage so much as a reminder of why my fear is unnecessary. Help me to see that even the worst thing that could happen to me today—my death— would mean a new and different freedom unlike any I have experienced before. "To live is Christ," we are told, and "to die is gain." Take away my fear and replace it with the certainty of your presence.

a prayer

for courage through god's presence

✛

I have cast myself into the hands of almighty God.
PATRICK, "CONFESSION," 55

Be strong and courageous . . . for the LORD
your God goes with you.
DEUTERONOMY 31:6

One legend that has been passed down is the story of Patrick lighting the Easter Fire. Whether it happened just like this we can't be sure, but here's how it is told:

It was Holy Week, and this year, Easter coincided with the festival of Beltane, in which all fires in the land were extinguished under penalty of death. The druid priests would perform their rituals, lighting the High King's Fire, from which all other fires would be rekindled.

Sensing God's leading, Patrick chose to make a bold stand against the power of the druids. On the Hill of Slane, across the valley from the king's residence at Tara, Patrick held a midnight mass and lit a great Easter bonfire. Seeing Patrick's fire, the druids warned King Lóegaire, "If that light is not put out before dawn it will never be extinguished."

King Lóegaire, accompanied by his wife, took soldiers to the bonfire and demanded Patrick give account for himself. Patrick did so gladly, and before the night was done the king's wife had converted to Christ. Lóegaire sensed that Patrick could not be beaten by direct conflict, so he ordered Patrick to come to Tara the following day so that they could talk further.

The musical tune for the ancient hymn "Be Thou My Vision" is known as Slane. The lyrics to the song were written by Patrick's spiritual grandchildren, and they reflect his courageous heart. What bold task has God called you to? Pray for God's presence to bring courage today as you meditate on these lyrics:

Be Thou my vision, O Lord of my heart;
Naught be all else to me, save that Thou art;
Thou my best thought, by day or by night,
Waking or sleeping, Thy presence my light.

Be Thou my battle shield, sword for the fight;
Be Thou my dignity, Thou my delight;
Thou my soul's shelter, Thou my high tower:
Raise Thou me heavenward, O Power of my power.

High King of Heaven, my victory won,
May I reach Heaven's joys, O bright Heaven's sun!
Heart of my own heart, whatever befall,
Still be my vision, O Ruler of all.

A PRAYER
FOR THE TRINITY TO PROTECT US

✠

*I arise today through a mighty strength, the invocation
of the Trinity, through belief in the Threeness, through
confession of the Oneness of the Creator of creation.*
"PATRICK'S BREASTPLATE"

*One of the teachers of the law came and heard them
debating. Noticing that Jesus had given them a good
answer, he asked him, "Of all the commandments,
which is the most important?"*

*"The most important one," answered Jesus, "is this: 'Hear,
O Israel: The Lord our God, the Lord is one. Love the Lord
your God with all your heart and with all your soul and
with all your mind and with all your strength.'"*
MARK 12:28-30

atrick's most famous prayer is known by several different names. Some call it "Saint Patrick's Breastplate" (for it was a prayer of protection). Others call it the Lorica (a Roman word for "armor"). It is sometimes called "The Cry of the Deer," because one story says God made Patrick and his monks appear as a herd of wild deer, allowing them to escape undetected.

While we don't know for sure whether Patrick or one of his students wrote this prayer, we do know that it reflects the values and heart of Patrick, and it's always included in the stories about him.

The morning after the Easter Fire, or so the story is told, Patrick set out for the Hill of Tara, the seat of the High Kings of Ireland. It was there that Lóegaire reigned, the king who was both fierce and fiercely opposed to Patrick's God. Lóegaire had sent druids to ambush Patrick and his followers on their journey, but the ambushers never saw the holy parade as it made its way to the king's seat.

Why were Patrick and his people hidden from those who would do them harm? Because, we are told, they had been praying "Patrick's Breastplate."

This prayer was purposely patterned on a traditional Irish incantation for protection on a journey. Patrick took this non-Christian tradition and infused it with the presence of Christian theology and references to Christ. So as we pray this prayer in the days to come, understand that Patrick is saying, essentially, "These truths about God are a protection

I am wearing on the journey I am on. They will keep me safe in the places I travel."

For today, let us pray with Patrick the first short stanza of "Patrick's Breastplate," which reminds us to take shelter in the presence of the Trinity: God the Father, God the Son, and God the Holy Spirit.

I arise today through a mighty strength,
the invocation of the Trinity,
through belief in the Threeness,
through confession of the Oneness
of the Creator of creation.

A PRAYER

✠

I arise today through the strength of Christ.
"PATRICK'S BREASTPLATE"

The angel said to them, "Do not be afraid. I bring you
good news that will cause great joy for all the people."
LUKE 2:10

For Patrick, the gospel was more than a theological construct; it was the good news of Jesus and what he had done for all of humanity. The story of Jesus gave him strength to get up in the morning, strength to stand up against those who opposed him, and courage to do things that others would call foolish: to return to Ireland, to criticize armed men who stole from his followers, and to go to the Hill of Tara and share the gospel with his greatest and most powerful adversary—despite not just the threats of death, but actual attempts on his life.

The good news brought joy for all people, for anyone who would listen to the message. That good news, which Patrick never tired of preaching to the people, was that Jesus Christ was God, come to earth as a human baby. That this same Christ had been baptized—a symbol of submission and obedience to his Father. That Christ had been wrongfully killed on a cross, buried in another man's tomb, and raised to life again by God. That he had ascended into heaven to make homes for his followers with God. And that he would one day return to the earth to bring justice for those who had been wronged and to punish evildoers: slavers and child killers and promoters of demonic religious practices, the wealthy who oppressed the poor, the rulers who thought only of themselves and never their subjects.

Can you think of a time when the good news you know about God in your life, or the story of Jesus, protected you? Whether from external forces or internal conflict, when has the good news kept you safe? Today, let us join Patrick in this section of the Breastplate prayer, where he prays to be strengthened by the story of Christ among us:

I arise today through the strength of Christ with His Baptism,
through the strength of His Crucifixion with His Burial
through the strength of His Resurrection with His Ascension,
through the strength of His descent for the Judgment of Doom.

A PRAYER
FOR THE SERVANTS OF GOD TO PROTECT US

*I arise today through the strength
of the love of Cherubim.*
"PATRICK'S BREASTPLATE"

*In speaking of the angels he says,
"He makes his angels spirits,
and his servants flames of fire."*
HEBREWS 1:7

atrick was no stranger to the spiritual world. God spoke to him in miraculous ways: through visions and dreams as well as through the unexpected words of friends and the glorious words of the Scriptures. Patrick shares of multiple specific attacks that were not from physical forces, but spiritual ones. He did not see the spiritual world as something separate from the physical, nor as something truly invisible, but rather something that we might choose to engage with—or not.

Though he had many enemies at many different times, Patrick remained convinced that his true enemy was spiritual. He did not remain angry at his former slave master, Milchu, but returned to him and shared with him the good news about Jesus. The great king Lóegaire, who tried to kill Patrick, was someone Patrick felt compassion for: Patrick shared the gospel with him many times, and when Lóegaire insisted he could not follow Jesus because his father would have refused to let him, Patrick only continued to pray.

Patrick didn't turn away from help in the spiritual realm. He prayed for God to send angels to protect him and his followers.

Patrick also sought God's protection in the community of fellow believers. He welcomed the prayers of leaders in the Church and took great pleasure in the assembly of the saints and of those young men and women of Ireland who had taken vows of chastity, devoting themselves completely to the work of telling others the good news, so that their countrymen might come to know God. He took great comfort in the great deeds done by those who did what was right, even when it was difficult.

The messengers and servants of God are all around us in the spiritual realm and the physical one. It is wise and good for us to work together with them and, as Patrick so often shows us, the first step in that process is often prayer.

Today, let us join Patrick's Breastplate prayer in asking for spiritual help to come from all the servants of God.

I arise today through the strength of the love of Cherubim,
in obedience of Angels, in the service of the Archangels,
in hope of resurrection to meet with reward,
in prayers of Patriarchs, in predictions of Prophets,
in preachings of Apostles, in faiths of Confessors,
in innocence of Holy Virgins, in deeds of righteous men.

a prayer
for god's presence in creation to protect us

✠

I arise today, through the strength of Heaven.
"PATRICK'S BREASTPLATE"

Listen to this, Job;
stop and consider God's wonders.
Do you know how God controls the clouds
and makes his lightning flash?
Do you know how the clouds hang poised,
those wonders of him who has perfect knowledge?
JOB 37:14-16

There are those who feel uncomfortable with seeking God in nature—they worry that they will worship the creature instead of the Creator. But Patrick had lived six years with his only book the book of nature, his only reading what he saw in the rolling hills of Ireland, or in the fiery patterns of the night sky.

He felt the Spirit in the wind, Christ who is our foundation in the stones, God who lives in unapproachable light in the fire, and in the babbling brook or the thunderstorm he heard the voice of God. In nature he found evidence and reminders of the God who made nature, and there he grew and learned to hear from God whatever his circumstance. His prayers were crafted in the ranging journeys he took with his sheep, and it was there that God responded.

There is something powerful, too, in recognizing that Patrick saw God through nature, while the Iron Age druids saw something different: they saw nature as god, a powerful force that must be cajoled and obeyed. To them, human sacrifice was sometimes necessary to make sure that crops grew, that weather was mild, and that plagues turned away. The Irish had been taught to fear nature, to worship it, and to be subservient to it. But Patrick saw something else, something better, something more: nature was not something to fear. In nature we could see God, yes, because he had created it.

Wherever you are today, whether in the city or the country, on a farm or in an office, look for some small scrap of nature: a leaf, a patch of blue sky, a stone, a potted plant. What can you see about God in that small piece of his creation?

Today, let's join "Patrick's Breastplate" as he finds strength in the beauty and power of the world around him: a world that is brilliant and splendorous, and all in the control of the one who made it.

I arise today, through the strength of Heaven:
light of Sun, brilliance of Moon, splendour of Fire,
speed of Lightning, swiftness of Wind, depth of Sea,
stability of Earth, firmness of Rock.

A PRAYER
FOR GOD'S CHARACTER TO PROTECT US

✦

I arise today, through God's strength to pilot me.
"PATRICK'S BREASTPLATE"

You are my hiding place;
you will protect me from trouble
and surround me with songs of deliverance.
PSALM 32:7

There were times when Patrick was asked for bribes or blackmailed in exchange for the safety of his community. "Give us money and we'll keep you safe." There were people who threatened to harm or enslave him or his followers. It would have been easy to think that arming his people and training them to fight would be the best route, the easiest way to keep themselves safe.

But Patrick believed that—just as when he had been a slave—God was watching, and God could be trusted. And the greatest weapon in making Ireland safe was not money or swords. It was the good news. If the Irish people came to know God and came to be like God, well, then Patrick and his people would have nothing to fear from them. The transformation of the Irish would keep them safe and would protect many others as well: the enslaved foreigners and the children who might otherwise be sacrificed to pagan gods.

We are tempted to find security in worldly things: jobs and paychecks, guns and locks, security guards and police officers. But all those things are nothing if God is not protecting us. Some people may trust in those things, but Patrick trusted in God alone.

By knowing God better, we learn more about his character, and the more we know his character, the more certain we are of his goodness, his power, and his love for us and humanity. Today let us pray from "Patrick's Breastplate" this section that emphasizes the person of God as the best way to be secure and cared for:

I arise today, through God's strength to pilot me:
God's might to uphold me, God's wisdom to guide me,
God's eye to look before me, God's ear to hear me,
God's word to speak for me, God's hand to guard me,
God's way to lie before me, God's shield to protect me,
God's host to secure me.

A PRAYER
AGAINST THE TEMPTATIONS
AND POWERS OF THE EVIL ONE

✠

God's host to secure me: against snares of devils,
against temptations of vices, against inclinations of
nature, against everyone who shall wish me ill.
"PATRICK'S BREASTPLATE"

When you pass through the waters,
I will be with you;
and when you pass through the rivers,
they will not sweep over you.
When you walk through the fire,
you will not be burned;
the flames will not set you ablaze.
ISAIAH 43:2

Patrick wasn't afraid to pray with great specificity about the troubles that faced him, and in today's prayer from "Patrick's Breastplate," we see him pray for protection from the supernatural and natural worlds, from powers and principalities and people who would harm him or his people.

He prays against false prophets and witches and warlocks and smiths (blacksmiths were seen as powerful magicians in those days), as well as against specific modes of death: poisoning and drowning, burning and wounds. Some of these things may seem far off to us today, people or situations we would be unlikely to run across. But what Patrick was praying about were the most obvious, most concerning forces in opposition to him in his everyday life.

So as we pray these specifics today, feel free to add in those powers and forces that oppose you in your daily life, those sicknesses you fear, those things which endanger your body or soul. We know that God is stronger than cancer or automobile accidents, bigger than politics, more powerful than any who might stand against us as we serve the Lord.

God's host to secure me:
against snares of devils, against temptations of vices,
against inclinations of nature,
against everyone who shall wish me ill,
afar and anear, alone and in a crowd.
I summon today all these powers between me (and these evils):
against every cruel and merciless power
that may oppose my body and my soul,
against incantations of false prophets,
against black laws of heathenry,
against false laws of heretics, against craft of idolatry,
against spells of witches and smiths and wizards,
against every knowledge that endangers man's body and soul.
Christ to protect me today against poison,
against burning, against drowning, against wounding,
so that there may come abundance of reward.

A PRAYER
FOR THE PRESENCE OF CHRIST

✠

Christ with me, Christ before me,
Christ behind me, Christ in me.
"PATRICK'S BREASTPLATE"

Where can I go from your Spirit?
Where can I flee from your presence?
If I go up to the heavens, you are there;
if I make my bed in the depths, you are there.
If I rise on the wings of the dawn,
if I settle on the far side of the sea,
even there your hand will guide me,
your right hand will hold me fast.
PSALM 139:7-10

hese may be the most famous lines from "Patrick's Breastplate." They have been adapted in other songs and prayers, and they have been quoted and sung and prayed for hundreds of years. At the core of these words is the deeply Patrician awareness of our need for God, and God's willingness to be present with us.

As he wrote these phrases, Patrick may have had in mind the apostle Paul's encouragement from the book of Romans: "Neither death nor life, neither angels nor demons, neither the present nor the future, nor any powers, neither height nor depth, nor anything else in all creation, will be able to separate us from the love of God that is in Christ."[10]

Patrick first invites Christ to accompany him, surround him, and indwell him. As Patrick himself is filled with Christ's love, he asks that Christ would shine through his words and deeds so that everyone he meets would experience God's presence for themselves.

Let's pray together:

Christ with me, Christ before me,
Christ behind me, Christ in me,
Christ beneath me, Christ above me,
Christ on my right, Christ on my left,
Christ in breadth, Christ in length, Christ in height,
Christ in the heart of every man who thinks of me,
Christ in the mouth of every man who speaks of me,
Christ in every eye that sees me,
Christ in every ear that hears me.

A PRAYER
FOR GOD'S SALVATION

✚

Salvation is of the Lord. Salvation is of Christ.
May Thy Salvation, O Lord, be ever with us.
"PATRICK'S BREASTPLATE"

Truly my soul finds rest in God;
my salvation comes from him.
PSALM 62:1

P atrick prayed for God to save him many times in his life. He prayed to be saved from slavery, from the cold, from illness that came from living out-doors in inclement weather, for deliverance and safe travels, for food when there was none to be found.

He was enslaved once as a boy but captured several times during his years as a missionary in Ireland. At this time people with money or more might have felt they could do what they wanted to people without power. Patrick lived through shipwrecks and plots against his life. Violence, targeted against him or his people, was something that happened many times.

Not only that, but there was his spiritual salvation. In later years Patrick looked back on his captivity with some sense of thankfulness, for it was during that time that he realized that he had been in spiritual captivity when he ran from God. "It was [in Ireland] that the Lord opened up my awareness of my lack of faith. Even though it came about late, I recognised my failings. So I turned with all my heart to the Lord my God, and he looked down on my lowliness and had mercy."[11] Patrick's literal slavery revealed his spiritual slavery, and he found salvation in spiritual realms before being set free in physical ones.

To pray for salvation is to acknowledge that we are in danger, that we are captives, that we are broken. It is in the presence of God (who is three in one) that we find salvation. Salvation is of the Lord.

Where do you need God's saving power today? What spiritual or physical or emotional needs do you have today? Let's take those to God as we pray.

I arise today through a mighty strength,
the invocation of the Trinity,
through belief in the Threeness,
through confession of the Oneness of the Creator of creation.
Salvation is of the Lord.
Salvation is of the Lord.
Salvation is of Christ.
May Thy Salvation, O Lord, be ever with us.

A PRAYER
FOR THOSE WHO DO NOT KNOW GOD

✢

*Our God is the God of all things, the God of heaven
and earth and sea and river, the God of sun and
moon and all the stars, the God of high mountains
and lowly valleys.*
"SAINT PATRICK'S CREED"

*[Jonah] answered, "I am a Hebrew and I worship
the LORD, the God of heaven, who made the sea
and the dry land."*
JONAH 1:9

There is a story that Patrick met two of the king's daughters, Ethna and Fidelm. It's said that these two daughters of Ireland asked Patrick many questions: "Who is your God? Where is he? Does he live in heaven or earth or under or in it? Is he in the streams or the mountains or the glens? Does he have sons and daughters, and are there gold and silver and other good things in his kingdom? How is God seen, how loved, how found? Is God young or old? Is he beautiful? Does he have a son, and if so who is he? Did his son live with God, or was he fostered? Does God have daughters, and are they dear and beautiful?"

Patrick's answer is sermon and song, poem and prayer. As we pray these words today, let us remember all the sons and daughters of this world who do not know God, and pray that they may find the God who is God of all things.

Our God is the God of all things, the God of heaven and earth and sea and river, the God of sun and moon and all the stars, the God of high mountains and lowly valleys. Our God is the God over heaven and in heaven and under heaven. God has a home in heaven and earth and the sea. He inspires all things, he gives life to all things, he is above all things, and sustains all that there is. It is he who lights the sun and brightens the moon. He made clear water flow in the desert and dry islands appear in the sea, and stars he made as ministers. His son is coeternal with him, like him, but not younger than him, nor is the Father older than the Son. And the Holy Spirit breathes in them and proceeds from them. Father and Son and Holy Spirit are not divided, they are one. How I want to unite you, too, to the Son of the heavenly King, so that you may be God's daughters and not only the daughters of an earthly king![12]

A PRAYER
FOR WHEN ACCEPTING A LEADERSHIP ROLE

✢

I declare that I, Patrick—an unlearned sinner
indeed—have been established a bishop in
Ireland. I hold quite certainly that what I am,
I have accepted from God.
PATRICK, "LETTER TO COROTICUS," I

I am the least of the apostles and do not even deserve
to be called an apostle, because I persecuted the
church of God. But by the grace of God I am what
I am, and his grace to me was not without effect.
I CORINTHIANS 15:9-10

God was doing something beautiful among the people of Ireland. The prisoners were set free, the blind made to see, those in darkness saw a great light. These people told their friends and neighbors and kin, and so the Church in Ireland grew. There were children who grew up to be priests and nuns, young men and women who took on the holy orders. Once, twice, and then many times

Patrick baptized a child who grew to follow God with their whole heart. There was a new generation of Irish who had known nothing other than this new Christianity, bright and green and growing. One day a messenger came with word for Patrick: the Church leadership back home knew there needed to be a bishop for the people of Ireland, and they had chosen this humble, earthy, unlearned sinner—Patrick. He embraced the messenger with great joy, and laughed at the surprising work of the God who saved him.

There are many places we are invited to lead: our families and workplaces, our churches and neighborhoods. Sometimes we might feel unworthy, and other times we may feel overlooked. Whatever the case, we know this: leadership is a responsibility and a grace given to us by God. We would do well to use it wisely.

We know, O God, that every authority on earth reports at some point to the Highest Authority. Teach me to be obedient to those in authority over me, and a joy to those who sit under my leadership. Give me a spirit of boldness, of kindness, of right judgment, and let me never use my position or power for my own good, but rather for the good of others. Give me clarity and strength, your insight, and clear certainty of what is right and how best to follow you. Thank you for this opportunity to accept greater authority to better serve my little ones.

A PRAYER
FOR WHEN FACING FALSE ACCUSATIONS

✣

They brought up against me after thirty years
something I had already confessed before
I was a deacon.
PATRICK, "CONFESSION," 27

Whoever touches you touches the apple
of [God's] eye.
ZECHARIAH 2:8

The accusations came years after Patrick's return to Ireland. Not when he was initiated into the priesthood. Not when he signed up as a missionary to Ireland, or when he was appointed as bishop. It was years later, after he had become well known for the work God was doing among the Irish people, that the accusation arose, eventually becoming a formal inquiry with his superiors.

It wasn't, of course, that Patrick had never sinned. But this accusation was based around a sin he had committed and repented of when he was fifteen years old. It had been brought to light by a childhood confidant. Now people were claiming he wasn't fit to lead. They talked about bringing him home—something he would have welcomed once, but now it filled him with dread. He couldn't leave his people behind.

Patrick spent hours in prayer, seeking direction. Perhaps this was God calling him back to his homeland? Maybe there was a deeper sin in his life he needed to acknowledge?

In prayer the Spirit acknowledged Patrick's pain and assured him God knew what was happening—that God saw the jealousy in those who were accusing him. God brought to Patrick's mind the Scripture, "Whoever touches you touches the apple of my eye." Patrick was precious to God. God would protect him.

We can become obsessed with protecting our own reputations, but in the end we can't control what others think of us—true or false. There is value in speaking truth at such a time, but when that is done, we must, like Patrick, turn it over to God and trust the Lord to keep us safe.

God, thank you for giving me strength in all things. I give you my anger and fear. I trust you to keep me safe in this time of uncertainty, and I trust that you will keep my reputation intact despite this slander. You have said that I am the "apple of your eye"—that if someone touches me with ill intent it would be like sticking their finger in your eye. Help me to respond with honesty, with integrity, and with grace. And you, O Lord, bring justice where it is due, and give mercy where you desire.

A PRAYER
FOR WHEN FACING BETRAYAL FROM A FRIEND

✠

How could he then afterwards come to disgrace
me in public before all, both good and bad, about
a matter for which he had already freely and
joyfully forgiven me, as indeed had God,
who is greater than all?
PATRICK, "CONFESSION," 32

After saying these things, Jesus was troubled in his
spirit, and testified, "Truly, truly, I say to you,
one of you will betray me."
JOHN 13:21, ESV

The false accusations could only come from one person, for Patrick had only ever told one person. They had played together as children, and their reunion when Patrick had returned from slavery had been one of great joy!

What confusion Patrick felt when he heard that this old sin had resurfaced. How could his friend have told someone else? He had trusted his friend with his very soul, and this was the result. It was this same friend who had been bursting with excitement when he told him, "Patrick, they are making you a bishop! Bishop of all Ireland!"

What jealousy, what pettiness could have caused him, then, to share Patrick's private past? Why would Patrick's friend wish to disgrace him? Patrick still remembered sharing his sin, and how his friend had said to him in that moment, "This action has been forgiven by God and by me." Now it seemed those words hadn't been true.

If these accusations had come from another person, they might not have stung so sharply. Patrick feared not only the loss of his reputation, or of his place with the people of Ireland, but also the loss of a dear friend who had meant so much to him.

Forgiveness doesn't mean, necessarily, a return to life as usual. We don't know whether Patrick's friendship was ever the same. We do know that he shared his deep hurt with God, and let Jesus bring truth and justice to the situation.

Forgive me my trespasses as I forgive those who trespass against me. My heart struggles to extend forgiveness to this dear friend who has betrayed me—yet how can I deny forgiveness to a friend who has hurt me, when you, O Lord, have forgiven me so much? In the midst of it all, God, I remain thankful to you. You have protected me from worse things than this. And here I am, still faithfully in your service. I turn this friend over to your loving hands to do as you see fit. Lord, speak peace to the turmoil raging in my soul.

A PRAYER
FOR OVERCOMING FEAR OF MAN

✤

*I have long thought to write, but up to now I have
hesitated, because I feared what people would say.*
PATRICK, "CONFESSION," 9

*We can confidently say,
"The Lord is my helper;
I will not fear;
what can man do to me?"*
HEBREWS 13:6, ESV

From a credential standpoint, Patrick did not stack
up well against other Church leaders. His education
was deficient, his Latin clunky, and his résumé was
not prestigious. Ireland was the frontier, his converts barbarians. Patrick knew he was considered by many to be a rustic.

So when the accusations started to fly among the bishops
on the continent, in a moment that called for decisive action,
Patrick hesitated.

Now years into his ministry, Patrick and the Church in Ireland were being attacked—not by druids—but by a fellow Christian. One of Patrick's colleagues had grown jealous as he watched the Irish Church flourish and Patrick outshine him. So he publicly condemned Patrick as unfit for ministry, digging up old sins and leveling accusations of corruption and greed.

When we think of heroes of faith like Patrick, we tend to visualize them as ever-confident and full of boldness. It's important to remember they are human. Remember Moses begging God to send someone else to lead the Israelites? How did God respond to Moses? *Moses, I am the one who made you and called you. I will equip you for the tasks ahead.*[13]

When you find yourself hesitating in fear, remind yourself of these truths that inspired Patrick, who trusted his spirit to the most faithful God, who served as ambassador to Ireland in spite of his shortcomings, because God doesn't use the world's standards in such matters. God chose Patrick for the job—Patrick, one of the least of God's servants, to be God's assistant.

Lord, sometimes you seem distant, and the voices around me seem much nearer and louder. I'm afraid to speak out, afraid to disappoint. I'm afraid of what others might do, say, or think. Let me hear you speak today: "You are My beloved child, in you I am well pleased." Secure me in your perfect love, and cast out my fears. Give me the courage and boldness to obey, listening to your voice alone.

*So I don't know which is the cause of the greatest
grief for me: whether those who were slain,
or those who were captured, or those whom
the devil so deeply ensnared.*
PATRICK, "LETTER TO COROTICUS," 4

The LORD is close to the brokenhearted.
PSALM 34:18

The soldiers had come during a baptism. There were children screaming, soldiers shouting, and Patrick yelling himself hoarse, trying and failing to prevent this from happening. And then it was over. Only corpses and mourners remained. He was numb with shock. The baptism had become a funeral.

Not only that, but the soldiers also kidnapped the women, planning to sell them. The soldiers had stolen everything of value, leaving behind only those whom they thought too damaged, too difficult, or too worthless to bother with.

Patrick's body was bruised. His chest hurt from sobbing, his face from being contorted in grief. There was anger and grief and sorrow. Fury at what had been lost. He could not find his way to the other side of this grief. It was too deep. Too complicated. Was he grieving for those who were murdered or enslaved? Was he grieving for the broken men who were so corrupted, so vile, that they could ignore their consciences and murder others for personal gain?

He didn't know. He only knew that this grief was too deep to get to the bottom of. Too heavy to be carried. Too wide to be crossed. In these days, so often when he prayed it was more groans than words.

Grief, once it arrives, does not leave us. But when we bring it to God, he grieves with us. He helps us to learn to carry it, and he comforts us.

Mary and Martha both once said, "If you had been here, my brother would not have died,"[14] *but how can I say that, Lord? I have seen you too often and too clearly to think that you weren't here. I know that you are present and you are always with me. I know you are good, I know you are powerful, and I know you could see what was about to happen, that in some sense you allowed this. I know you see how broken I've become, that my heart is not only broken, but crushed. I know that in time you will teach me how to carry this pain, but I honestly cannot see my way from here to there. I'm sitting down in the ashes to wait for you. I can't walk another step. I can't get to you, Lord, so please, come to me.*

✠

So the injuries done to good people will not please
[God]—even in the very depths it will not please.
PATRICK, "LETTER TO COROTICUS," 12

Those who oppose the LORD will be broken.
The Most High will thunder from heaven;
the LORD will judge the ends of the earth.
1 SAMUEL 2:10

These soldiers who had murdered the people of God, kidnapped others, and stolen their belongings were commanded by a man named Coroticus. He threw lavish parties with his ill-gotten gain, promised protection, invited people to feasts. To Patrick's astonishment there were people who went. Christian people, who pretended Coroticus and his men had not become wealthy through the murder and enslavement of other Christians,

127

would attend his parties. They became his friends. They asked to be part of his inner circle.

Didn't they understand that people like Coroticus and his soldiers would meet justice one day? One couldn't please Coroticus and also please God.

Patrick wrestled with his anger. He wrote a letter to Coroticus and sent it along with a brave priest, whose face shone with righteous anger as he marched to the soldiers' camp. Patrick had known this young priest since he was born, had seen him grow up—wonder of wonders!—in an Irish Christian home. Praise God! And Coroticus and his men laughed at this priest, this miraculous man of God who had been born here, on this island. At least they didn't kill him.

The world is full of evil people, malicious people. Too often we are their victims. Some well-meaning ministers tell us to forgive and forget, but must we forget if there has been no justice? Even in the Bible, God's people ask for justice. They demand it. "How long, O Lord, holy and true, until you will bring justice on the earth?"[15]

God's justice too often moves slower than we think it should, so our prayers for justice (for others) must often be accompanied with prayers for patience (for ourselves).

What am I to do, Lord? I am greatly despised. Your sheep around me are mangled and preyed upon. Thieves have descended on the flock. Evil-minded people have murdered and stolen and abused us. Help me keep my mind from fantasies of revenge against these evil people. Teach me to forgive, if such a thing is possible. But I pray that you will not forget this terrible wrong, Lord. Instead, may your righteous justice roar like mighty water and wash these evil people away. It is not my job to bring justice, but yours. Give me patience to see your judgment come.

A PRAYER
IN TIMES OF WEEPING

✠

*I do not know what to say, or how I can say any
more, about the children of God who are dead,
whom the sword has touched so cruelly. All I can
do is what is written: "Weep with those who weep";
and again: "If one member suffers pain, let all
the members suffer the pain with it."*
PATRICK, "LETTER TO COROTICUS," 15

Jesus wept.
JOHN 11:35

Weep with those who weep.

His sheep did not want answers. Maybe
they would in time. As shepherd now his role
was only to walk among his people, to see them weeping, to
sit beside them and together let the tears roll, their shoulders
shaking, their chests tight with grief, wailing and mourning
and shouting in often wordless grief.

Words were of little use for the mother whose daughter had been stolen away.

A sermon would mean less than nothing today to someone whose brother had been cruelly gutted by a sword.

The grandmother who had lost son and daughter-in-law and three grandchildren did not care to have him sing a hymn or recite Scripture.

So they wept. They wept until they could weep no longer, until their throats hurt and their lips cracked and their red eyes dried not from healing but from lack of moisture. Then they slept.

But Patrick lay awake. He lay awake and wept and prayed.

We're tempted in terrible times to jump to the triumph in our future: one day Jesus will bring justice on the earth! But that day is not today. We must be careful not to minimize our losses by failing to grieve. Jesus wept when he knew Lazarus would be raised from the dead in a matter of minutes! And for us, our losses will last years, not minutes. We must learn to weep when it is time to weep.

I have no words. No words, only tears. Tears enough to drown a nation, tears enough to fill a new sea. God, I am not asking for you to give me an explanation, not even asking for you to give me comfort. I only ask that you would sit beside me here, that I would know that you, too, see the horrific sorrow that is in this world, and that you would weep beside me. That would be enough, O Lord, that you would weep with me.

A PRAYER
OF COMPASSION FOR EVIL PEOPLE

✣

*However late it may be, may they repent of acting
so wrongly, the murder of the brethren of the Lord,
and set free the baptised women prisoners whom
they previously seized. So may they deserve to live for
God, and be made whole here and in eternity.*
PATRICK, "LETTER TO COROTICUS," 21

*Love your enemies and pray for those
who persecute you.*
MATTHEW 5:44

atrick had forgiven his slave master. At the time,
that had seemed to him the greatest thing that
would ever be asked of him. How small an injustice that seemed today, when soldiers had murdered his
beloved congregation and carried away the young women
to be slaves.

Patrick realized that the greatest revenge would not
be for these evil men to be tortured or maimed or killed.

The greatest revenge would be for them to recognize their own sin. If they came to truly know God, the pain they had caused would become their own. They would wail for forgiveness then.

In his best moments, Patrick didn't wish revenge at all. He didn't wish for these poor deceived soldiers to come to God so they would suffer. No, he knew that if they would come to God, they would experience something beautiful: the healing presence of God. They would be made whole, in this life and the next.

Patrick had been deceived once too. God had lit a great bonfire in that darkness. Patrick knew there was forgiveness available to these men. Had not Saul been forgiven? Perhaps one of these men would turn to God and become a great missionary of the Church. On his best days, Patrick prayed that they would see God.

The path to forgiveness cannot be climbed by force of will. We require God to lift us along the way. After we grieve, the next step toward forgiving others is asking God to teach us to do it.

Lord God, the people who have done me harm are also made in your image. They've hurt people I love, they've sinned, they've done such deep damage to my life that I despair of being able to find true forgiveness for them. And yet they have been lied to, abused, and broken by the world as well. How sad that they are so far from truth. So I ask with true desire: Let them see you, God. Open their ears to hear your voice. Soften their hearts to understand your good news. You don't call me to heal people who are already well. Give me strength to love them, and may each of them come to know you, that their lives may be filled with joy.

A PRAYER
FOR PERSEVERANCE

✠

*I pray that God give me perseverance, and that he
grant me to bear faithful witness to him right up to
my passing from this life, for the sake of my God.*
PATRICK, "CONFESSION," 58

*Keep a close watch on yourself and on the teaching.
Persist in this, for by so doing you will save
both yourself and your hearers.*
1 TIMOTHY 4:16, ESV

Even after all these years—all the sorrows and hardships and troubles and joys and celebrations and baptisms and funerals and weddings and christenings—Patrick sometimes worried about his flock wandering after some other shepherd. Although soldiers and bitter persecutions and the bloody death of their fellow congregants hadn't scared them away, there was one thing he worried could destroy their faith.

If Patrick himself became unfaithful—through temptation, through sin, through sheer exhaustion or grinding fatigue—would they walk away from God too? And though Patrick would later come to be called a saint, he never thought of himself that way. He knew he was the least of those who followed Christ, a humble servant of God, and there were times when the fear of falling away from God seized his heart and he shook with despair.

Still, if he feared his own weakness, he put his faith in God's strength. He couldn't be certain of keeping himself to the narrow path, but he could trust that God would. We, too, may come to moments when we cannot see a clear way to continue to follow God in the way we know God desires. On those days we can join Patrick in asking for God's strength to persevere.

Almighty God, I fear I might wander from your path if I rely on my own strength. I need your supernatural power to give me perseverance. Grant me the power to be faithful not just today, not just tomorrow, not just next week or next month, but until I take my final breath. May those who look up to me as a spiritual example never be given cause to doubt that you are a great and powerful and loving and compassionate God. Give me perseverance for the road ahead of me, God. Guide my feet and give me strength.

A PRAYER
FOR BEING HONEST ABOUT ONESELF

✛

Although I am imperfect in many ways, I want my
brothers and relations to know what I'm really like,
so that they can see what it is that inspires my life.

PATRICK, "CONFESSION," 6

Create in me a clean heart, O God,
and renew a right spirit within me.

PSALM 51:10, ESV

Thousands of people became followers of Christ through Patrick's ministry. Brothers came from elsewhere in the Church, wanting to know what he was doing to make this happen: Was he praying more? Was he more insightful, a harder worker?

But none of those things were true.

Whole villages asked him about the true God. Young men and women came from across Ireland and asked to become monks and nuns. This was a movement of God, not some genius spirituality from Patrick.

In fact, Patrick had plenty of failings. There were days when he struggled with anger . . . at those who persecuted his flock, at himself, even at the messages that came from people back in the place he had once called home. There were days when God spoke and Patrick didn't want to do what he had been told. Sometimes he snapped at people when he was hungry. Kindness came to him through hard work and discipline.

How had these thousands come to Christ? In the same way Patrick had—through a loving voice speaking to their hearts. Sometimes they heard this voice in the words of Patrick, but that was not because of him. He was only an obedient servant. When he was honest about his own shortcoming, then people saw the work of God more clearly. This was something he worked to make sure remained true.

We are tempted, sometimes, to hide our broken places, to pretend we never mess up or make a mistake. But when we are honest about our failures, others can see God more clearly in our lives.

God, help me to see myself clearly, and to never think more highly of myself than I ought. Likewise, prevent me from thinking I am less than you have made me to be. Teach me to be honest with those around me, that they might see clearly the places where your light shines through in my life. I am imperfect in many ways—let others see that you delight in using the weak so that we might more clearly see your strength.

A PRAYER
FOR THE PEOPLE OF GOD

✠

*I pray for those who believe in
and have reverence for God.*
PATRICK, "CONFESSION," 62

*I pray for them. I am not praying for the world,
but for those you have given me, for they are yours.*
JOHN 17:9

P atrick knew all too well the cost of following Jesus. It was a life of willing servitude not only to God, but also to his neighbor and even to those who had wronged him. To follow Jesus meant caring for those God cares for, and for him that had meant learning to care for his kidnappers, his master, and the people of Ireland.

He knew God would ask similar things of his Irish converts. The act of having one's heart changed, the transformation that follows, is an act that creates discomfort and pain.

He felt true compassion for those who believed in God and would follow God's paths and commands.

Not that it was without joy to follow God! Patrick had more joy than could be contained in his heart, and it spilled out into the lives of the people around him. How pleased he was to see the captives freed, the terrified lean into God's love, and the sick and wounded healed and made whole.

How often he wanted to take them in his arms and protect them from every harm that could come! But he knew, too, that they needed to grow and become dependent on God, not on him.

There are so many things outside of our control, and so many moments when our loved ones can be hurt by the world or even because they are following God. In those moments we must ask for God to heal not only our broken places but also those of our friends and loved ones.

You are called the Great Physician, and well you should be, for who else can heal not just the body but the soul, not only broken bones but also broken spirits? I have many friends who have chosen to follow you, and I keep coming back to this same prayer over and over: teach them to be one with one another in the same way you are one, God. Help us to love one another, to serve one another, to be deep in one another's lives. And those wounds that we cannot heal on our own or for our friends—well, Lord, we turn those over to you, that you might heal us in your time.

A PRAYER
OF REPENTANCE

✠

I know to some extent how I have not led a perfect
life like other believers. But I acknowledge this to
my Lord, and I do not blush in his sight.
PATRICK, "CONFESSION," 44

I finally admitted all my sins to you and stopped
trying to hide them. I said to myself, "I will confess
them to the Lord." And you forgave me!
All my guilt is gone.
PSALM 32:5, TLB

P atrick knew the journey to repentance well. How often did someone ask him about this? How often did they struggle to understand? They came from a religion of terror, so they expected God to stand over them in fearsome anger, demanding their subservience.

Patrick taught them another way. Bring your wrongdoing to God. Tell God your every imperfection; he already knows them all. Don't blush, don't stammer, don't fear. God loves you, and that perfect love casts out fear.

When you come close to God, don't expect judgment, but rather forgiveness. And *repentance*—that strange religious word—means only to make the decision to never again do the wrong thing that you had brought to God. How often he explained this to his flock, and how often he modeled it in his own life! Did he pray a prayer of repentance every day? Perhaps not. But he knew that he could—that he likely should. He still tried to hide his failings sometimes, like a child hiding his face behind his hands, thinking his parent could not see him. But on his best days he ran to Christ, joyous, to share his many failings and receive in exchange a reminder of God's forgiveness, God's generosity, God's love.

Reflect on your week. What moments of failure do you see? Where could you have been kinder, more loving, more like God? Where do you see good moments, when you were truly like the Lord? Let's ask God to make us more like Jesus.

O Lord, I have become aware of something you already know: a moral failing in my life. A wrong I have done. A sin. There is a part of me that feels shame bringing this to you, and another part that fears telling you what I have done. This is not who I desire to be. I bring this brokenness to you and ask that you would forgive me and give me strength to never do this thing again. Teach me to walk in your truth. Forgive me, Lord, and take away my sin. I turn away from that sin and toward you, and the righteous path you have set before me.

a Prayer
for Leaving a Legacy

✤

After my death I may leave something of value to
the many thousands of my brothers and sisters.
PATRICK, "CONFESSION," 14

One generation will praise Your works to another,
And will declare Your mighty acts.
PSALM 145:4, NASB

Patrick was closer to the end than he was the beginning. He had been serving in Ireland for decades now. He had no children, no home, no wealth or possessions to speak of. He had left his parents and family behind. Was it worth it? No part of the journey had been easy—he faced conflict, danger, and temptation even now—but many parts had been deeply rewarding.

Especially gratifying were the relationships he had built, and the lives he had seen transformed. Patrick writes with joy of the sons and daughters of kings who turned from idolatry to love God and their fellow countrymen. He speaks of the poor and the slaves who now gratefully served a new Master. Though he felt the weight of his personal sacrifice, he knew that he was leaving behind a legacy with his spiritual children that would continue with the new generation.

In the final paragraph of his letter, Patrick focuses his gaze even farther forward, to generations long unborn. He reflects on the amazing transformation that happened in Ireland, and prays for us, the readers of his letter, that we would give credit not to Patrick, but to Patrick's God, the giver of all good things: "I pray for those who believe in and have reverence for God. Some of them may happen to . . . come upon this writing which Patrick, a sinner without learning, wrote in Ireland. . . . It was a gift of God."[16]

When your journey is over, how will you be remembered? Whether you are "significant" in the eyes of the world, whether you have many children or none, we all have opportunities to make lasting investments in those around us and to point them to the one who loves them and ever lives for them.

Lord, help me to live my life today in light of eternity. Show me opportunities to share your love and make a difference, not to build my own name, but for your glory and the joy of your creation.

a prayer

for saying goodbye at the end

✠

*I testify in truth and in great joy of heart before God
and his holy angels that I never had any other reason
for returning to that nation from which I had earlier
escaped, except the gospel and God's promises.*

PATRICK, "CONFESSION," 61

*I have fought the good fight, I have finished the race,
I have kept the faith.*

2 TIMOTHY 4:7

It was a mild day in March, and Patrick—an old man now—climbed to where he could see the ocean. He needed his staff to make his way on a cliff like this, a cliff he would have bounded over like a lamb in his youth. The sounds of waves on the black rocks and seabirds echoing across the coast comforted him now, when so long ago they had been reminders of what trapped him in this place.

He was not a perfect man. He had sinned. There were also moments when he had done the right thing—to all outward appearances the actions of a holy man—and his motives had been mixed or even impure. There were times he had sinned in his actions, or had sinned in his heart. But had not the Great and Glorious One still used him? Had not thousands been baptized, and many more who had heard the great and precious promises of God?

A shepherd stood nearby, keeping watch over his flock. Patrick smiled to himself and pulled his cloak tighter around his thin shoulders. His whole life he had been a shepherd too. First for sheep that were not his own. Then for these people, the harassed and helpless, the lost and lonely, the precious and beloved people of Ireland. And they were not his sheep, no, they belonged to God, but he had come to love them as he loved his Master. In the end he could say with full honesty and no regret: everything he had done here had been because of the promises and good news of God. He had done his best, all that he could do, and left the rest to the power and mighty arm of the Lord.

A bell tolled somewhere on the island, and his heart swelled with joy. What he wouldn't have given as a child to hear the bell of a church in the pagan land of his captivity! Now he heard them every day. He closed his eyes to pray. The waves, the seabirds, the bleating of the sheep, the call of the shepherd, and now the bell of the church. It was enough. The years of sacrifice, the fear, the hunger, the bone-chilling cold, had all led to this moment—his sheep, well cared for and fed. He had not lost a single one of the little ones who had been given into his hands.

His smile broadened as he stepped out of Ireland for the last time, and into his Master's house.

One day we, too, will come to the end of our journey here, and enter into our true home. Like any journey there are preparations to be made, goodbyes to be said, old parts of our lives to be left behind. May the Lord grant us that we, like Patrick, might make that final journey with no regrets.

Lord God, the time has come to say goodbye to many things, and many people. I am thankful for those who have loved and blessed me on my journey so far. I am sorry for those whom I have harmed along the way. Thank you for these people whom you gave into my care. I did my best by them, and in my heart I wanted to bring them only good things: your good news, your promises. I led them to green pastures and beside the still waters. I watched over them as best I knew how, and now I turn them over to you, the Good Shepherd, knowing that you will care for them better than I ever have.

A FINAL PRAYER

As we end this prayer journey with Patrick, we thank you for his example and the lessons we have learned praying alongside him. And as he has entered into your heavenly Kingdom, we pray alongside him still today, praying for the people he so dearly loved: O Father, protect the children of Ireland. O Lord, bless the women of Ireland. O God, turn the hearts of the Irish men toward you. Amen.

acknowledgments

MATT AND AARON:

Many thanks to Sarah Atkinson for seeing the power in Patrick's life of prayer and giving us a chance to write this book. To Sarah Parker Rubio and Debbie King for helping us shape our ideas to be the best they could be. And to Wes Yoder, who has been a champion along the way for this book and for us!

AARON:

Thank you, Matt, for jumping into this project with me—a first time writer—and for walking with me through life's challenges as we wrote together. Thank you to my wife, Andrea, for believing in me and journeying with me through each adventure! Thank you to my kids (Anthony, Micah, Ellie, Julia) for both giving me time to write, and pulling me back into your world so I can stay a kid at heart.

MATT:

As always, huge thanks to my wife, Krista, and my kids, Zoey, Allie, and Myca, all four of whom bring me joy and gratitude on a daily basis. Many thanks also to my parents, Pete and Maggie, and my parents-in-law, Janet and Terry. And, of course, huge thanks to my dear friend Aaron Burns. Thank you for inviting me on this journey!

NOTES

1. Matthew 6:9-13, kj21.
2. Patrick, "Confession," 1.
3. See 2 Peter 3:8.
4. See Galatians 5:1.
5. 1 John 4:18, esv.
6. See Proverbs 21:1.
7. See Matthew 28:19.
8. See Mark 16:15.
9. See Romans 9:25.
10. Romans 8:38-39.
11. Patrick, "Confession," 2.
12. "Saint Patrick's Creed."
13. See Exodus 4.
14. See John 11:21, 32.
15. See Revelation 6:10.
16. Patrick, "Confession," 62.

ABOUT THE AUTHORS

Aaron Burns is a film producer, director, and writer with a passion for timeless storytelling. He recently directed *Birthright: Outlaw and Legacy Peak* for Sony Affirm. His producing credits include the record-setting *Beyond the Mask* and the number one box office hit *War Room*. Aaron lives in Michigan with his wife, Andrea, and their children.

Matt Mikalatos is an author, screenwriter, and speaker. He's the author of *Journey to Love* and the YA fantasy series The Sunlit Lands. He has written for Today.com, *TIME magazine*, *Relevant*, *Nature*, *Writer's Digest*, and *Daily Science Fiction*, among others.